# IS-794: External Affairs Program Liaison

## By

## Fema

11/13/2013

# Lesson 1:

# Communication Challenges in a Disaster

## Course Welcome

The purpose of this course is to prepare trainees to serve in Program Liaison positions within the Planning and Products component of External Affairs (EA).

The Program Liaison's primary function is to interface with programs at the Joint Field Office (JFO), gathering information that EA may use in communications that support the disaster response and recovery operation and advising all program areas of the ways in which External Affairs can support their activities.

This course provides an overview of the Program Liaison's responsibilities, identifies challenges that must be overcome, and suggests strategies to succeed.

## Course Objectives

At the end of this course, you should be able to:

- Recognize the importance of getting accurate and timely information that informs the general public and survivors to the public during and after a disaster.
- Explain how the Program Liaison supports the disaster recovery mission by gathering and sharing information.
- Describe techniques for building and maintaining effective working relationships with program areas.
- Describe how information gathered by the Program Liaison is analyzed for significance and to identify opportunities to achieve mission objectives.

## Lesson Overview

This lesson explores the importance of getting accurate and timely information to the public during disaster recovery operations.

Upon completing this lesson, you should be able to:

- Describe why information is so important in a disaster and the repercussions when communication breaks down.
- Identify common barriers to communication in a disaster.

# Imagine It Has Happened to You

Imagine that the hurricane that has been threatening your community has just made landfall. It changed direction overnight and now is headed directly for you.

You and your spouse have been listening to the radio and hear the warning to evacuate NOW! You grab your daughter and leave for a friend's home where you hope to be safe from the storm.

Now imagine it is 2 days later and you want to come home, but you are unsure if it is safe to return.

Listening to the news from your friend's home, the coverage is focusing on the most damaged areas and your community isn't mentioned. You read about road closures in the paper, but one TV station says the roads are now open. The county Web site says that only limited access is being granted and homeowners without a valid reason to come home are being turned away.

Your coworker tells you that everything is destroyed and looters are roaming the streets.

As you begin the drive home, you are not sure how far you will get before being turned around or what you will see when you get there. You hear on the radio that FEMA will be coming to town and bringing help to people in the declared area.

You wonder: What kind of help is being offered and what kind will I need? What does declared area mean? Is this help for me and how do I get it? But most of all, you wonder if your home, your possessions, your photos, and other treasured mementoes will even be there when you arrive.

Now imagine that you need to communicate vital recovery information to the person who has experienced all of this. What message will you send? What words will you use? How will you get the message to them? What challenges will you face?

This course will address the challenges of communicating in a disaster and the role of the Program Liaison in overcoming these challenges.

By learning and using these techniques, you will play a crucial role in helping people recover from life-changing disasters and start a new day.

# What Happens When Communication Breaks Down

When people don't have access to credible, accurate, and timely information in a disaster it creates a void. All too often, that void is filled by speculation, rumor, and half-truths.

Decisions that are made based on unsound information are likely to be bad decisions. In a disaster, a bad decision can threaten personal safety and hinder the disaster response and recovery effort.

# What Could Possibly Go Wrong?

In the absence of good information, people may:

- **Do the wrong thing,** such as evacuating when it is safer to shelter in place.
- **Fail to do the right thing,** such as not applying for assistance because they do not know they are eligible for help.
- **Do the right thing in the wrong way,** such as making home repairs before the damage has been assessed or making the repairs in an unsafe manner.

With good information, people are able to make good decisions and contribute to the disaster recovery.

# Creating Confidence in Government Response

Good information also contributes to a successful outcome by promoting confidence in the people and organizations involved in disaster recovery.

Disaster survivors can trust what they hear if the source has credibility. And, if they trust what they hear they are less likely to be influenced by rumors.

# Communication and Credibility

The government and nongovernmental organizations involved in the disaster recovery earn the public's confidence by providing information that is timely, accurate, meaningful, and understandable. When the message is lacking any of these three characteristics, a credibility gap is created.

And, once credibility is lost, it is difficult to regain.

# Communication Model

At the most basic level, communication can be illustrated by this graphic.

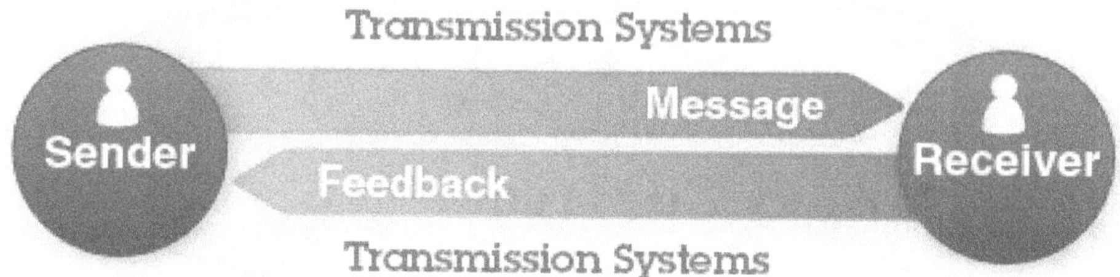


A sender sends a message to a receiver using various systems of transmission. The receiver gets the message and demonstrates in some way (provides feedback) that the message was received. This feedback may or may not be transmitted through the same systems.

# The Communication Model in a Disaster

In a disaster requiring a coordinated Federal response, the sender in our illustration is Emergency Support Function (ESF) 15 External Affairs. The receiver includes all of the diverse audiences that External Affairs serves and, ultimately, the disaster survivor and the public. The message(s) will be related to disaster recovery (e.g., how to apply for assistance). The transmission systems will include the news media, town-hall meetings, and face-to-face delivery of verbal and written messages.

When disaster strikes, it affects every aspect of the communication model.

# Sender Problems That Hinder Communication

The sender—in this case, those in the government charged with communicating with the public in a disaster—may be hampered in their efforts because:

- The situation is evolving so information is rapidly changing.
- Those in command have priorities other than information sharing, so not enough information is available.
- Time constraints make collection of data and analysis of information a challenge.

# Transmission System Breakdowns

In a disaster, systems that normally facilitate communication may be unavailable or incapacitated; for example:

- Power may be completely or partially out.
- Public information avenues (e.g., newspaper, radio, television) may be down.
- Community gathering places for information sharing (e.g., places of worship, community centers, schools) may be destroyed or temporarily closed.
- Road closures may prevent face-to-face visits.

# Receiver Problems Related to Disaster Communication

During and after a disaster, the receiver of the message may experience difficulties accessing and absorbing information. Disaster victims are often:

- Confused and anxious about the situation.
- Unsure who or what to believe.
- Distracted by multiple, conflicting messages from numerous sources.
- Challenged by personal needs related to language preferences or access or functional needs (e.g., visual or hearing impairments, cognitive difficulties, etc.).

All of these problems make it difficult for the receiver to understand incoming information.

# Addressing Communication Challenges

Merely clearing away barriers is not enough to ensure good communication. The multitudes of issues that arise in a disaster require the sender to analyze the information needs and prioritize messages accordingly. This analysis and prioritization of messages is accomplished through ESF 15.

# Lesson Summary

In this lesson, you learned about communication challenges during and after a disaster and the impact they can have on people and on the recovery effort.

In the next lesson, you will learn how FEMA addresses communication challenges in a disaster through ESF 15 External Affairs and the Program Liaison's role in that operation.

# Lesson 2: Program Liaison Role in Improving Communication

## Lesson Overview

This lesson presents an overview of ESF 15 External Affairs and describes how the Program Liaison supports the disaster recovery mission by gathering and sharing information.

Upon completing this lesson, you should be able to:

- Describe the ESF 15 External Affairs functional organization in a disaster.
- Describe how the Program Liaison function provides a vital communication link between External Affairs and the rest of the disaster recovery organization.

## ESF 15 Overview

Emergency Support Functions (ESFs) are groups of government and private-sector resources organized under the National Response Framework (NRF) to provide coordinated Federal response to an incident.

ESF 15 External Affairs is charged with providing information to affected audiences.

## A Cohesive Approach

ESF 15 External Affairs is:

- Sharing information, sharing resources, and providing all audiences with a single, unified message.
- A national model, but emulated by many States, tribes, and localities.
- A strategy that is integrated, comprehensive, and empowered.
- Activated by the ESF 15 External Affairs Director.

# Role of FEMA in ESF 15

The NRF identifies the Department of Homeland Security as the Coordinator of ESF 15 and DHS/FEMA as the Primary Agency charged with executing the function.

The overall purpose of ESF 15 is to provide accurate, coordinated, timely, meaningful, and understandable information to affected audiences, including governments, nongovernmental organizations, the media, the private sector, the general public, and disaster survivors.

# Standard Operating Procedures

The ESF 15 Standard Operating Procedures (SOP) provide tactical guidance and organizational recommendations for incidents requiring a coordinated Federal response.

The SOP addresses the roles and responsibilities of all government and nongovernmental organizations involved in ESF 15 and applies to incidents regardless of the size or complexity.

In executing ESF 15, the Federal External Affairs team is guided by the principle of "maximum disclosure, with minimum delay."

# ESF 15 in the Field

The Federal Government establishes and conducts External Affairs activities in the field through coordination with the affected State, local, territorial, and Tribal partners. This unified operation includes the following functions:

| External Affairs Officer | <ul><li>Appointed by the ESF 15 Director (DHS Assistant Secretary for Public Affairs).</li><li>Manages External Affairs resources according to the Incident Action Plan (IAP).</li><li>Establishes strategies and tactics to meet incident objectives.</li><li>Oversees External Affairs functions.</li><li>Establishes and communicates basic work procedures.</li></ul> |
| --- | --- |

| Resource Support | <ul><li>Oversees and manages all product, equipment, and contract needs of ESF 15 (e.g., satellite trucks, translation services, advertising).</li><li>Provides day-to-day support for space and equipment needs.</li></ul> |
|---|---|
| Planning and Products | <ul><li>**Role:** To coordinate and develop all communications plans and materials for the disaster operation.</li><li>**Primary Customers:** All entities involved in the disaster operation, including program areas, other Federal and NGO agencies, and EA components.</li></ul> |
| Joint Information Center | <ul><li>**Role:** To coordinate incident information, public affairs activities, and media access to information regarding prevention, preparedness, response, recovery, and mitigation.</li><li>**Primary Customers:** News media.</li></ul> |
| Intergovernmental Affairs | <ul><li>**Role:** To coordinate the exchange of incident-related information between FEMA and local, tribal, and State officials.</li><li>**Primary Customers:** Local officials, including mayors, council members, supervisors, city/county clerks; tribal leaders; State legislators; and others.</li></ul> |
| Private Sector | <ul><li>**Role:** To coordinate with business networks and industry-specific groups on incident-related issues that directly affect the private sector.</li><li>**Primary Customers:** Private sector entities affected by the incident.</li></ul> |
| Congressional Affairs | <ul><li>**Role:** To coordinate the exchange of incident-related information between FEMA and Members of Congress and their staffs.</li><li>**Primary Customers:** Members of Congress and their staffs.</li></ul> |

# Planning and Products

Let's look closer at Planning and Products—the component that includes the Program Liaison function. Planning and Products:

- Develops communication products for external and internal audiences.
- Develops and directs all strategic planning and messaging for the JFO.
- Provides coordinated communication links with program areas and others involved in the recovery.

| | |
|---|---|
| AEAO P&P | Manages the Planning and Products component of External Affairs; reports to the External Affairs Officer. |
| Creative Services Manager | Manages the Creative Services function. |
| Research and Writing Specialist | Produces written material for internal and external audiences. Products for the news media include news releases, media advisories, fact sheets, etc. Products for other audiences include talking points, flyers, and briefing books for VIP tours. |
| Speaker's Bureau | Coordinates speaking engagements with news media, town hall meetings and other events for all areas of the JFO. |
| Limited English Proficiency/Additional Communication Needs (LEP/ACN) Specialist | Addresses special communications needs and supports all components. |
| Strategy and Messaging Specialist | Develops plans for clear and consistent communication of operational messages. Requires absorbing and analyzing large quantities of information to identify trends and implications and anticipate issues. |
| Program Liaison Manager | Manages the Program Liaison function. |
| EA Reports Specialist | Assembles content into prescribed formats to meet External Affairs' reporting requirements. |
| EA Program Liaison Specialist | Provides communication links with assigned disaster recovery program areas:<br><br>• Individual Assistance<br>• Public Assistance<br>• Mitigation<br>• Other Federal, State, and voluntary agencies<br>• Disaster Recovery Centers |

# Program Liaison Function

Program Liaisons are assigned to program areas—such as Individual Assistance, Public Assistance, and Mitigation—and other Federal, State, and voluntary agencies at the JFO. Program Liaisons work from their assigned program area to:

- Develop disaster situational awareness about the assigned program area.
- Gather information from the assigned program area on developing issues and intended strategies to address these issues.
- Identify trends and analyze information for External Affairs implications.
- Provide advice on how External Affairs can help the program area achieve success.

# What You Bring to the Table

Program area experts are responsible for complex, multifaceted disaster programs. They also know their audiences, whether they are disaster survivors or affected local governments.

What program area experts may not know—but you can tell them—is how External Affairs operates and what services and resources External Affairs can bring to the table to help them achieve their disaster recovery objectives.

| | |
|---|---|
| Media Outreach | Includes development of news releases, talking points, and coordination of media interviews; also includes support at events that may attract the media (e.g., town hall meetings, public assistance briefings, Disaster Recovery Center operations). |
| Internet Coverage | Includes placement of messages on FEMA and disaster-specific Web sites, including those maintained by State partners and other Federal and nongovernmental organizations. |
| Social Media Content | Coordination with FEMA Headquarters staff to disseminate messages via social media. |
| Printed Materials | Development of a variety of printed materials, including flyers, posters, and brochures. |
| VIP Tours and Media Ride-Alongs | Coordination of VIP tours involving local groups (e.g., Governor's Office and State legislators, business officials, |

| | and congressional representatives); ride-alongs with the news media to view specific disaster recovery operations. |
|---|---|
| Special Events | Includes External Affairs supports at special events (e.g., mitigation workshop with local home improvement store), especially those that will attract media interest. |
| Photo and Video Documentation | Includes documenting damage and activities related to program areas as well as creating public service videos to promote the recovery effort (e.g., mitigation success stories). |
| Translation Services | Coordination of translation services at program-area events for non-English speaking audiences or those who have difficulty hearing. |

# Characteristics for Success

The successful Program Liaison demonstrates:

| **Critical listening skills:** | Use active listening and open-ended questions with program experts to fully understand the issues and build a good base of knowledge. |
|---|---|
| **Ability to extract and interpret information:** | You will take in voluminous amounts of information. Your ability to consolidate and put the information into words the target audience will understand is the value you bring to the program area. And, some of what you will hear is not for public dissemination; handle sensitive information with discretion. |
| **Perseverance:** | Invest in developing a constructive relationship with the program experts. It may take a while (or a try or two) to convince them of the benefit of working with External Affairs, but it will be worth the effort. |
| **Relationship-building skills:** | Build trust with program staff by meeting your commitments, showing respect and a willingness to learn, and demonstrating your expertise. |
| **Strategic thinking:** | Anticipate potential issues and advise program staff on implications and strategies. |

# Words of Experience

**Barbara Ellis:** As Program Liaison you have to gather a lot of information, process that information, and be prepared to brief that information with each of your External Affairs components. This requires critical listening skills but also knowing where to go to get the most accurate and thorough information.

Building relationships in a program area is essential for a Program Liaison. Knowing as much as you can about the program area you are assigned to will help bridge those relationships and build trust and confidence on behalf of External Affairs. Get to know the subject-matter experts within their fields that will provide you with critical information and analysis when you need it.

**Michelle Block:** Serving as the link between the program area and External Affairs, there is a two-way information flow. As Program Liaison, you can identify any "red flags" that arise from the program and provide the External Affairs perspective, letting them know when a decision might have repercussions that External Affairs support can help mitigate.

It is key to build positive relationships with the program staff and support External Affairs' credibility with our internal partners. For example, providing a preliminary review of news releases for program information before it goes to the program area, streamlining the number of times we reach out to them for routine items.

**Ricardo Zuniga:** Program areas can be pretty close-knit and you may find yourself ignored or left out. Don't be thin-skinned and don't take it personally. Perseverance is the key. You can become successful by convincing them that you are there to help THEM succeed. What is crucial is the Program Liaison's ability to take in the facts, consolidate the information, and make it understandable. This is what helps the program area and serves the disaster survivor.

**Leslie Lillard:** As a Program Liaison you take in a massive amount of information and it is very easy to get wrapped up in the details of issues. Each day, or several times a day, it is important to step back and ask: Am I seeing the big picture? What am I missing? Am I considering all the players?

Additionally, building a sound relationship with program partners is key to success. Don't be discouraged if a program area doesn't readily welcome you. They may not have an understanding of what exactly you're doing. Educate them on how your work can benefit theirs, and demonstrate that ability. If you can take someone's misperception of what EA does and make them a fan, you've turned a substantial challenge into an opportunity for success!

# Lesson Summary

In this lesson, you learned about ESF 15 External Affairs and how the Program Liaison improves communication by representing External Affairs in assigned program areas.

In the next lesson, you will learn how the Program Liaison must develop strong relationships with the program areas to be successful as a representative of and advocate for External Affairs.

# Lesson 3:

# Building and Maintaining Relationships

## Lesson Overview

This lesson describes the importance of building and maintaining effective working relationships with program areas in the Joint Field Office (JFO) and the advisory role of the Program Liaison as the representative of External Affairs.

Upon completing this lesson, you should be able to:

- Describe why positive working relationships are crucial to performing the Program Liaison function.
- Describe barriers to building relationships with program areas in the JFO.
- Describe techniques Program Liaisons can use to build and maintain positive working relationships with program areas.
- Describe how Program Liaisons can advise program areas in how they can work with External Affairs, and the benefits they can receive as a result.

## Good Relationships – Why They Matter

It's not enough to be technically competent to do your own job. Because no one can be successful working alone, interpersonal skills make the difference between success and failure. Good working relationships lead to:

- Full utilization of expertise and ideas.
- Improved collaboration and teamwork.
- Improved efficiency and utilization of resources.
- Higher job satisfaction.

## Importance of Relationships to the Program Liaison

The Program Liaison's role is to be the link between program areas in the JFO and External Affairs.

It would be impossible to do that job successfully without first establishing good working relationships both with the program area staff and with the External Affairs staff.

# Barriers to Building Relationships

The JFO and disaster recovery environment create significant challenges to building and maintaining positive working relationships. The Program Liaison needs to recognize these challenges and adopt techniques for overcoming them. As Program Liaison, you must overcome:

- Lack of time.
- Lack of understanding.
- Lack of trust.

# Barrier #1: Lack of Time

The JFO and disaster recovery environment is marked by long hours, hectic activity, and high-stress atmosphere. It takes time to develop good working relationships, and in the JFO, there is often not enough time to get to know people well in a relaxed atmosphere before diving into critical work.

Additionally, JFO assignments may be short in duration, and with each deployment new working relationships must be built.

# Barrier #2: Lack of Understanding

It takes two to build a relationship. If the program area staff does not understand the value of External Affairs, they will be less motivated to develop a solid working relationship with the Program Liaison.

As Program Liaison, you can educate the program area on the opportunities and benefits afforded by working with External Affairs. In other words, answer the question: What's in it for me and what's in it for my stakeholders?

# Barrier #3: Lack of Trust

Relationships start with trust. If a program area feels it has been "burned" before, the staff is less likely to fully welcome an outsider into their day-to-day activities and discussions. The problem may have started with negative media coverage or a miscommunication with External Affairs from a previous disaster.

It doesn't matter that the problem did not involve you; as Program Liaison for the current disaster, you will still need to overcome any negative history to earn the program area's trust.

# Techniques for Building and Maintaining Relationships

As Program Liaison, you will co-locate with the assigned program area in the JFO. This proximity increases your ability to gather information, but coming into another's workspace makes it more important than ever to start off on the right foot.

You can make a good first impression by showing respect for coworkers, demonstrating a professional demeanor, keeping your commitments, and displaying a positive attitude.

Now let's look at two important tips for building and maintaining strong relationships with program areas.

# Tip #1: Do Your Homework

Before taking your seat in your assigned program area, prepare yourself by doing some research. The following resources will help you begin developing situational awareness:

- **Incident Action Plan** documents incident objectives and overall strategy; it also includes key people and issues related to each program area.
- **Situational Report (SitRep)** reports current status of the recovery operation, including details related to each program area.
- **Strategic Communication Plan** identifies External Affairs objectives and strategies in line with the Incident Action Plan.

# Tip #2: Learn and Respect the Program Culture

Every group of people develops its own culture. In the workplace, this culture is reflected by spoken or unspoken ground rules. For example, are meetings started promptly or do you wait for all to show up? Is it okay to use someone else's workspace or equipment without asking or not?

Another part of culture relates to social time. Does the group regularly gather for meals or does everyone go off on their own?

You will find it easier to develop relationships if you observe the program area's expectations for workplace culture. Make yourself a part of the group!

## Educator and Advisor Roles

In addition to gathering information from program areas and reporting back to External Affairs, the Program Liaison plays an important role as educator and advisor.

Some program staff will be quite astute in how and why External Affairs does what it does. Others will benefit from your expertise as you explain External Affairs' role in the recovery operation and suggest ways that External Affairs can help them accomplish their goals.

## Relationships With External Affairs Staff

You may be working out of the program area's office space, but you are still part of External Affairs, and good relationships with your colleagues are crucial to your success.

Take full advantage of hotwashes and other meetings to keep abreast of what is going on in External Affairs and to share what you have learned.

Getting together for dinners or after-work social activities can also keep you an active member of the group.

## Lesson Summary

This lesson explored the importance of building and maintaining relationships with program areas and identified barriers that can hinder these relationships in the disaster recovery environment. The lesson also covered techniques for overcoming some of these barriers and maximizing these relationships.

In the next lesson, you will learn how the Program Liaison can identify and take advantage of opportunities to use External Affairs strategies to benefit program areas and the disaster recovery mission.

# Lesson 4:

# Identifying and Seizing Opportunities

## Lesson Overview

This lesson describes how information gathered by the Program Liaison is analyzed and used by External Affairs to further the disaster recovery mission.

Upon completing this lesson, you should be able to:

- Describe the kinds of information Program Liaisons may gather from program areas.
- Describe how Program Liaisons analyze information by determining the significance and relevance for External Affairs.
- Describe an eight-step communication model used to plan, implement, and evaluate External Affairs activities.

## What the Program Areas Do

As Program Liaison, you will be assigned to program areas that can be quite complex:

| Individual Assistance | Programs are available to help people recover from disaster in a number of ways, including:<br><br>• Individuals and Households Program that provides:<br>    o Temporary housing.<br>    o Repairs to make disaster-damaged homes livable.<br>    o Replacement housing.<br>    o Permanent housing construction.<br>• Other Needs Assistance for individuals who are uninsured or underinsured and unable to meet disaster-related expenses to pay for such things as medical and dental care, funeral costs, transportation expenses, etc.<br>• Disaster Case Management that ensures the sequence of delivery is followed to streamline assistance, prevent duplication of benefits, and provide an efficient referral system. |
|---|---|

| | |
|---|---|
| | <ul><li>Crisis Counseling to relieve grieving, stress, or mental health problems related to a major disaster.</li><li>Other Assistance, including:<ul><li>Disaster Unemployment Assistance</li><li>Disaster Legal Services</li><li>USDA Disaster Assistance</li><li>Veterans Affairs Disaster Programs</li></ul></li></ul> |
| Public Assistance | Programs to help governments and certain nonprofit organizations recovery from disaster include assistance to:<br><br><ul><li>Remove debris.</li><li>Repair public buildings, roads, bridges, and other infrastructure.</li><li>Perform certain emergency protective measures.</li></ul> |
| Mitigation | Programs to reduce the risk of future disaster damage include:<br><br><ul><li>Hazard Mitigation Grant Program, which provides grants to implement long-term hazard mitigation measures.</li><li>National Flood Insurance Program (NFIP), which allows insurance companies to provide flood insurance in communities that participate in the NFIP.</li></ul> |

# Understanding the Information You Gather

SitReps can report numbers of registrations for disaster assistance and can tell you the status of debris removal. Media analysis reports can reiterate what the news media is saying.

But it is your experience and insight—applied to what you learn from your assigned program area—that deepens the value of the information you gather.

| | |
|---|---|
| Individual Assistance | <ul><li>Details on housing needs and teleregistration statistics that may not be fully explained in the SitRep.</li><li>Anecdotal information from staff outside the Joint Field Office (e.g., staff at the Disaster Recovery Centers (DRCs) and operators taking registrations for disaster assistance).</li><li>Relationships with the State and localities.</li><li>Immediate priorities.</li></ul> |

| | |
|---|---|
| | - Potential or developing situations.<br>- Changes in policy or procedures from Headquarters. |
| Public Assistance | - Details on public assistance projects not fully explained in the SitRep, including debris removal and infrastructure repairs.<br>- First-hand observations from staff working in the field.<br>- Relationships with the State and localities.<br>- Immediate priorities.<br>- Potential or developing issues.<br>- Changes in policy or procedures from Headquarters. |
| Mitigation | - Mitigation projects from previous incidents (where they are and how successful they have been).<br>- Relationships with the State and localities.<br>- Immediate priorities.<br>- Potential or developing issues (e.g., NFIP status of affected localities). |

# Analyzing Information for Significance

As Program Liaison, you will collect and interpret voluminous amounts of information. Your first objective is to analyze the program information you hear to evaluate its importance.

This analysis starts by determining the significance of the information to the mission. Ask the program experts and ask yourself:

| | |
|---|---|
| **What is the magnitude of the issue?** | - How many people will be affected?<br>- How large is the affected area?<br>- How long will the repair/recovery/work take? |
| **What is the impact?** | - Is this an objective in the Incident Action Plan?<br>- How will this affect the disaster survivor?<br>- How will this affect the ability to achieve the disaster recovery mission? |
| **How timely is the issue?** | - Has this already happened?<br>- Is this imminent? |

| | |
| --- | --- |
| | • Do we have lead time to prepare? |
| **Who is involved?** | • Does this involvement impact the disaster survivor? <br> • Does this involvement impact the State? <br> • Does this involvement impact other partners in the recovery effort? <br> • Does this involvement impact other program areas? |

# Analyzing Information by External Affairs Relevance

Once you have identified a significant issue or activity, the next part of the analysis is determining its relevance. Ask yourself: Is this an opportunity for External Affairs support?

In most cases, you will report out during hotwashes or directly to your supervisor (Program Liaison Manager or Assistant External Affairs Officer – Planning and Products). This is the time for you and others to evaluate the potential opportunity in the context of everything External Affairs is doing, the objectives in the Strategic Communication Plan, and the resources available.

# Sharing Your Expertise To Maximize Opportunities

In some cases the program expert may know what is needed and ask you to write talking points and coordinate an interview with the media. Based on previous experience, he or she knows this is something External Affairs can do and that it results in a better interview.

In other cases you will need to be the advisor/advocate for External Affairs, pointing out opportunities to the program expert and suggesting ways in which External Affairs can help.

This proactive role is one of the most valuable contributions the Program Liaison can make to the disaster recovery.

# Eight-Step Communication Model

FEMA Headquarters has adopted an eight-step communication planning model based on the concept of strategic messaging. This model can be used to plan an overall External Affairs program or to support a single activity.

This method of communication planning allows the Program Liaison to support the program areas and to feed information into the Strategic Communications Plan developed by External Affairs. The information helps build, modify, and evaluate the plan.

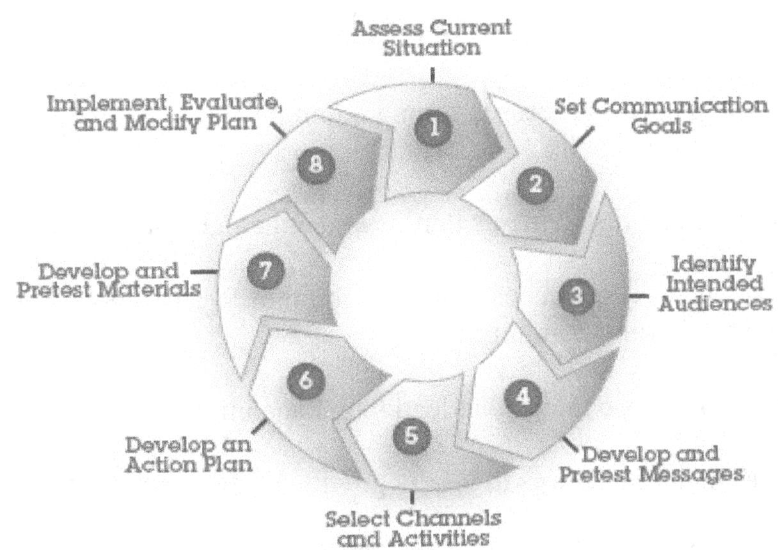


# Step 1: Assess Current Situation

This step sets the stage for the entire process and should be done in collaboration with the program area subject-matter experts. In this step, you need to collect information that answers the questions:

- What is the FEMA communication need you want to address?
- Who are the people that are most affected by this problem?
- What actions could your audience take to address this problem?

# Step 2: Set Communication Goals

The next step in this process is setting communication goals and objectives that are realistic and measurable.

**Goals** can be broad statements that describe the purpose and meaning of the task.

**Example:** Increase awareness and utilization of Ready.gov to promote mitigation and preparedness in rural communities.

**Objectives** are those things that lead to the accomplishment of your goals.

**Example:** Increase visitors to Ready.gov by 5% by next month.

NOTE: The SMART acronym is used by many organizations. FEMA uses the "SMARTS" acronym with the final "S" standing for "strategic."

# Step 3: Identify Intended Audiences

It is important to work with the program area to identify the target audience. The program experts will have real insight into their audiences and will help you to get a detailed understanding of who you want to reach.

For example, the Public Assistance program expert (and Intergovernmental Affairs staff) will be able to tell you that different mayors in the same State or region can be concerned with different things:

- Mayor Smith: Reelection
- Mayor Jones: Budget
- Mayor Jacobsen: Gang violence

# Step 4: Develop and Pretest Messages

Messages can be:

- Informative: Telling people about FEMA's role as a coordinating organization rather than an emergency responder.
- Persuasive: Getting people in San Francisco to be prepared for an earthquake.

- Both: Persuading people that preparedness is their responsibility, and also giving them specific information about how they can be prepared.

**Characteristics of Effective Messages**

Effective messages:

- Are succinct.
- Use no jargon.
- Are easy for your audience to understand.
- Are direct and concise.
- Are credible.
- Humanize the subject.
- Move beyond the **features** of the work (what you do; how you do it).
- Communicate the **benefits** to your audience (the positive results from the audience's perspective; answer the question: "What's in it for me?").

# Step 5: Select Channels and Activities

As Program Liaison, you are in a unique position to make the link between the program area's needs and External Affairs' goals and objectives, but you need to collaborate to get the full picture.

Identifying the best avenues for delivering your message should be done in cooperation with others in External Affairs. This avoids scheduling conflicts, duplication of effort, and conflicting messages. It also ensures that needed resources will be available.

# Step 6: Develop Action Plan

Use an action plan to determine where, when, how, and by whom each task will be completed to successfully implement your activity. This plan can be as simple as a short list that includes tasks, target dates for completion, and the person responsible for ensuring each task is completed. It should also identify needed resources.

An action plan keeps you on track and identifies what you need from the program area to get the job done.

# Step 7: Develop and Pretest Materials

Pretesting materials when you are working at the JFO may not seem practical or even possible, but it helps to understand and appreciate the process.

Pretesting of materials is conducted to make sure the targeted audience:

- Understands the message.
- Finds the material(s) credible.
- Responds positively to the graphic design.

# Step 8: Implement, Evaluate, and Modify Plan

Whether implementation involves issuing a news release or coordinating a VIP tour, the results should be evaluated and the "lessons learned" should be used to modify your plan of action for the next time.

Ideally, the program area should be involved in the evaluation and, along with External Affairs, answer these questions:

- Did we achieve our objectives? (This is why measurable objectives are so important!)
- What went well?
- What could we have done differently for better results?
- How can we build on this success?

# How Does the 8-Step Plan Fit In?

The 8-step model contributes to effective incident planning.

- The Incident Action Plan, External Affairs functional plans and Strategic Communications Plan are part of the overall incident planning.
- The 8-step is particularly well-suited to specific events and activities (e.g., VIP tour), but the broad concepts are relevant to other aspects of incident planning.

# Lesson Summary

In this lesson, you considered how the Program Liaison uses External Affairs expertise and program area knowledge to identify opportunities for External Affairs to support program area activities and the overall mission. The final step for the Program Liaison is to collaborate with the program area experts to evaluate what was done and build on success.